THE CELTS
IN CORNWALL

Henry Jenner

OAKMAGIC PUBLICATIONS 2001

THE CELTS IN CORNWALL

Henry Jenner

First published by Henry Jenner
Circa 1916.

This edition:

OAKMAGIC PUBLICATIONS 2001

ISBN: 1 901163 39 3

For a list of 80 titles on all aspects of Cornish
folklore & antiquities, send SSAE to the publisher.

Also by Henry Jenner:

King Arthur In Cornwall

OAKMAGIC PUBLICATIONS
2 SOUTH PLACE FOLLY,
PENZANCE TR18 4JB.

Visit our website at:

www.oakmagicpublications.com

Are you interested in Cornish folklore ?
Subscribe to our biennial journal:
THE CORNISH ANTIQUARY, published
in May and November. Articles on faery folk,
stone circles, Celtic & Cornish legends, etc.

INTRODUCTION.

THIS essay claims little or no originality. It only aims at putting in a short and fairly intelligible form for the benefit of the members of the Old Cornwall Societies a sketch of what is known about those nations that are called by the general name of " Celtic." If there is any *arrière-pensée* in it at all, it consists in a desire to show that Cornwall may reasonably claim to be counted as one of the Celtic nations, and that it has affinities and relationships, linguistic, ethnological and historical, with the other Celtic nations, and especially with Brittany, and to point out that Cornish people ought to recognise this in the present, as they undoubtedly did in the past.

Nationality, which not a very easy thing to define, does not necessarily depend upon language, race or political jurisdictions. The Basques, though united by very marked language and race, have little national consciousness, but are French or Spanish, according to which side of the Pyrenees they happen to be on. No one will deny that Switzerland is a nation, yet the Swiss have no language of their own, but speak, more or less correctly, French, German or Italian. Romansch, the fast dying speech of part of the Grisons, is no exception, for it is really a North Italian dialect spelt in more or less German fashion, and is not peculiar to Switzerland, and under the name of " Ladine " (i.e. Latin) it is spoken in parts of what was once Austrian, but is now Italian Tyrol. In blood the Swiss are probably largely Gaulish Celtic, that is to say, of the Aryanised " Alpine " race, with a considerable mixture of German (Burgundian, Allemannic and Swabian), and a dash of Hunnic, and they are a federation of varying jurisdictions, united under a central federal government. Yet they have as strong a national consciousness as any nation in the world. The United States of America, in blood a heterogeneous mixture of all the races of Europe with the additions of some of Africa and Asia, but having an English basis, with a language which is not peculiar to them, but is English of sorts, form a large, if not a great, nation, about whose obtrusive, not to say truculent national self-consciousness and also its power of absorbing immigrants there can be no doubt. Each of these has a clearly defined country of its own, which in neither case is part of a larger political jurisdiction which it shares with any other nation. He would be a bold man who should tell a Scotsman that Scotland was not a separate nation, and yet in it there are three languages, excellent English, usually spoken with something of an accent, a dialect of Northern English origin generally known as "broad Scots," and Celtic Gaelic, and two sets of very different racial characteristics, the Highland and the Lowland, and the whole country, though its ancient legal system is still preserved, is under exactly the same political jurisdiction as England, and has been so since May 1st, 1707. But though no part of the British Empire is more loyal (or more useful) to it than Scotland, there is no doubt about its separate national consciousness, in which Scottish Celt and Scottish Teuton unite as one homogenous whole. The Jews are undoubtedly a separate nation, though they have had no country for 1858 years, but only the memory of one, and no common language, for Hebrew, once no doubt their language, has not really been spoken by them since the Captivity (B.C. 588), and is only retained as a learned and liturgical language, like Latin in western Europe, while "Yiddish" is only bad German, with some mixture of Polish, Hebrew and Aramaic vocabulary, written in Hebrew letters. Scattered in every country of the world, under every possible sort of political jurisdiction, they are kept as a separate nation by race, religion, national characteristics and interests, and a very strong national consciousness. The Poles, united in language, mentality and religion, remained consciously a nation even when for considerably over a century they were under the three several jurisdictions of Prussia, Austria and Russia, and the ease with which recently the old Austrian Empire has been divided up into three new republics, while parts of it have been joined to Italy, Serbia, Poland and Roumania, shows that there was no sort of united national consciousness in that menagerie of races, languages and religions. The inhabitants were in the mediæval mental attitude of loyalty (or sometimes disloyalty) to a King, rather than patriotism to a country. Germany, in theory from the fall of the "Holy Roman Empire" in 1806, and in practice for very long before that, down to 1870 was a number of independent states, which could and often did make war on each other, each owed allegiance only to its own King, Elector, or Duke, and the

Reformation sorted them into two separate and often very hostile camps. Yet the inhabitants were all Germans together, and what national consciousness they had was German rather than Prussian, Bavarian, Saxon, Hanoverian and the rest. The same may be said of Italy from the break-up of the Western Roman Empire down to the "Risorgimento" of 1859-60 and its completion in 1870. In these two cases there was an internal national consciousness before there was externally a nation, and this was to some extent recognised by poets, such as Dante in Italy and Goethe in Germany.

It may be said that national consciousness is the most important factor in nationality, and that a community, however heterogeneous in language, race or religion, is a nation when it feels itself to be a nation, and the cause of that consciousness must be sought in history, sometimes, as in the case of the United States, in very recent history, sometimes in that of ancient or mediæval times. It is not easy to determine when the various kingdoms which arose on the ruins of the Roman Empire first acquired a conscious sense of nationality, but for a long time what attachment there was seems to have been personal to a prince rather than territorial to a country and the theory of the Feudal System preserved that aspect of allegiance to some extent as long as feudalism lasted. City States, such as Venice, Florence, Genoa and others in Italy and the Free Cities of the Empire, like the ancient Greek City States, attained in the early Middle Ages to what at first sight appears to be something like modern nationality, but the conception was in reality not so very different from that of the monarchical states, the republic, and largely in practice a more or less aristocratic oligarchy, taking the place of the prince. Perhaps the earliest modern manifestation of a sense of nationality, as we now understand it, was when in the late thirteenth and early fourteenth centuries the Forest Cantons round the Lake of Lucerne, the nucleus of the Swiss Federation, freed themselves from the dominion of the Hapsburgs, but the general mediæval feeling was, probably quite unconsciously, that the Roman Empire was not really dead, and that Western or Latin Europe, which included much that was Teutonic and had never been in the old Empire, formed a single whole, however much its component parts might quarrel or fight among themselves. In the minds of mediæval men Christendom was one, with the Empire, even the shadowy restored Empire of Charlemagne, for the body and the Church for the soul. Probably it may be held that among great nations the modern idea of nationality, now so universal, was first recognised consciously in England in early Tudor times, and that its development there was partly the cause and partly the effect of the Reformation. Certain it is that by the end of the Tudor period it was fully developed in England, and was beginning to take hold of other large nations also.

The Goidelic Celts, a term which is explained later on, continued in the tribal, patriarchal, or clan stage of development down to very modern times, and the clan sentiment is by no means extinct in the Scottish Highlands now. In the great war, Lord Breadalbane and the late Captain Douglas Campbell of Argyll raised a regiment of Campbells and Lochiel a regiment of Camerons without the slightest difficulty, and there were other instances also. It was the most natural thing in the world for the clansmen to " come out " when their chief called them. But the clan system, as its name implies,—*clann*, Welsh *plant* (with the usual change of *c* to *p*)=children— presupposes, actually or by fictions of adoption, a descent from a common and historically known ancestor, a blood-relationship, and the chief is simply the head of the family. This does not necessarily make for national consciousness, for though the chiefs might owe allegiance to some over-lord or King and, as in 1745, a large proportion of the clans might unite to fight for that King, that was the chiefs' and not the clansmen's business. It was not until about the end of the seventeenth century at the earliest that Ireland really awoke to the fact that it was a nation, though it had always recognised that it was Celtic, or at any rate not English. The Scottish Highlanders until the legal abolition of heritable jurisdictions and clanship after the '45 had very little sense of nationality, though no doubt they would have called themselves Scotsmen in a general sort of way. The unit was the clan, and each clan, though sometimes there were federations of several of them, was practically independent and the King's writ did not run in its country very much. Now their national consciousness is Scottish rather than Highland only, and they seem to count Scotland as a whole as a Celtic nation. As for the third Goidelic country, the Isle of Man, after being under the Saxon, Norwegian, Scottish and English Kings, it was made into a titular hereditary kingdom by Edward III in 1343 under the House of Stanley, with so much local autonomy as to be practically independent. Twice it was taken from the Stanleys but restored again, and after being inherited by the Dukes of

Atholl, the sovereignty was purchased by the English Crown in 1765. The local autonomy under a separate legislature still goes on, but there is little or no evidence to show the age or extent of any existing national consciousness.

The Brythonic Celts are those Celts whose ancesters had been Romans for some four centuries, and had then reverted to their original Celticism. In the beginning of this reversion and for some time after, what national consciousness they had was Roman rather than British, a consciousness of being by right citizens of the theoretically, and, as far as they knew, practically world-wide Empire. It was really cosmopolitism, a very different conception from the modern idea of nationality. Rome, though in its earlier days it had a sense of nationality and very absorbing patriotism not unlike that of modern times, when it became a world-Empire did not rule over conquered nations as an external power nor, like the British Empire, did it form a confederacy of states, but assimilated the countries which it annexed, so that in the Empire, to adapt St. Paul's words (Col. lll. ii) about the Church, there was " neither Greek nor Jew, Barbarian nor Scythian," but all were Romans together. Some, like the Jews and to some slight extent the Greeks, both of whom had once had something hardly distinguishable from the modern patriotic idea, though the Greeks had largely lost it, might hold out and refuse to be assimilated, but that was not the case with the Britons. These, however, had not been quite so much assimilated as the continental Celts, and when they ceased to be Romans they very soon began under external pressure to develop a rudimentary sense of nationality, perhaps at first directed towards a general British nation, but later towards the three jurisdictions into which that nation was divided. For a long time, indeed down to the union of Wales and Cornwall to England and of Brittany to France, the sentiment was indistinguishable from loyalty to kings, princes or dukes. The last attempt at the independence of Wales in 1402-15 was of this sort and was really a very nearly successful attempt to effect a restoration of Owain Glyndwrdu (generally known as Owen Glendower), the alleged descendant of the last independent Prince of Wales, Llywelyn ap Gruffydd, to the throne of his ancestors. How far he really was the legitimate representative of Llewelyn does not matter. He had first begun to make trouble in 1400, apparently to restore Richard II., supposed to be still alive, but the Welsh people believed Owain to be their rightful sovereign, and he was crowned as Prince at

Machynlleth in 1402. Probably it was after the failure of this attempt that under external pressure the Welsh, who submitted to the King of England, began to develop a conscious sentiment of nationality, apart from loyalty to a prince of their own. It was not until 1535-6 that the Palatine jurisdiction was abolished and Wales was incorporated into England, and this incorporation, which changed the status of the country from that of a principality separate from England, but under the same king, to that of a united kingdom of England and Wales, may well have had an effect, exactly the opposite of what was intended by Henry VIII., of intensifying the nascent national consciousness. In Brittany when it was first united to France there was for a time no conflict of loyalty, for the Duchess of Brittany having become Queen Consort of France, her son Henry II. peacefully and naturally suceeded to Brittany as well as to France, and so did his sons Francis II., Charles IX. and Henry III. A permanent union of the two crowns had been accepted by the States of Brittany in 1532, but when Henry IV., who was not the heir of the Duchy of Brittany, or a descendant of the Dukes at all, succeeded to the French crown in 1589, and was besides that a Protestant, Brittany revolted in favour of Isabel of Spain. grand-daughter of Henry II., who was the senior heir. After a desultory war of about nine years Henry IV., who had in the meantime become a Catholic, received the submission of the Duc de Mercœur and the rest of the Breton insurgents, and from that time forward none were more loyal subjects of the French Kings until the extinction of the French monarchy—and indeed for long after—than the Bretons. National consciousness and some amount of independence remained, though the object of Breton loyalty was a "foreign" sovereign, and down to the Revolution Brittany was governed by its own " Etats de Bretagne " under a military " Commandant-en-Chef " and a civil " Intendant," both representing the French King, who was also recognised as Duke of Brittany. It was nearly an analogous case to that of England and Scotland between the accession of James VI to the throne of England (as James I.) in 1603 and the union of the Parliaments of the two countries in 1707. Brittany was no more conquered or annexed by France than Scotland was conquered or annexed by England. The Revolution ended Breton " Home Rule," though not without a struggle, which on the Breton side was inspired by the mixed motive of loyalty, patriotism and religion, and even down to our own day Brittany was the stronghold of

Royalism. Whether any remains now "this deponent sayeth not," for he does not know, but until the death of Henry V. in 1883 Breton Royalism was a very real thing, nearly as real as Breton nationalism, which is as strong now as it ever was. It has had during the nineteenth century and after an immense accession of conscious national sentiment for various reasons.

The case of Cornwall differs from those of Wales and Brittany in many respects. It is not certain how or exactly when the old Cornish or Damnonian line of kings ended, but it was probably in the first half of the tenth century, and, except for the rather legendary Earl Condor at the time of the Norman Conquest a century and more later, no one ever even claimed to represent them. Therefore Cornish separate national sentiment, whenever it began to be recognised, never had in it any mixture of loyalty to a rightful sovereign, whether dispossessed or in possession, and it seems to have begun fairly early. There is little if any evidence of the attitude of the Cornish towards the Saxons kings from the early tenth century to the Conquest. It is perhaps significant that in the submission of Bishop Kenstec to the see of Canterbury in about 870, when a King of Cornwall was still reigning, he describes himself as elected to the episcopal see " in *gente* Cornubia " (in the nation of Cornwall) and that when Eadulf, Bishop of Crediton, was given three manors in Cornwall in 909 it was " ut . . . visitaret *gentem* Cornubiensem " (that he might visit the Cornish *nation*), while in Ethelred's charter cf 994, and often later, it is " *provincia* Cornubiæ." Something had changed the status between those dates. But this is only evidence of the Saxon attitude towards the Cornish. These would seem to have accepted the Norman kings without any question, and though it is alleged that Condor was deprived of his earldom of Cornwall by William I., it is by no means certain that he ever held it, there is no evidence that he had any Cornish adherents, and very little evidence, and that rather shaky, that he ever existed. From the Conquest right on through the Middle Ages the Cornish were loyal, even if sometimes disobedient, subjects of the Kings of England, but Cornwall was commonly counted and described as a separate country from England, though belonging to the same king. "Anglia et Cornubia" was as common an expression as "England and Wales" is now. There is not much mediæval evidence of what the Cornish thought of themselves as regards nationality, but a good deal to show that the English looked upon them as a separate nation. Even as late as about 1580 an agent of Philip II. of Spain describes them as differing entirely from the English in language, customs and laws. The Cornish risings of 1497, partly against burdensome taxation and partly in favour of the claim of Perkin Warbeck, and of 1548-9 against the religious changes were apparent instances of national self-assertion, and so too was the threatened rising in 1628, which, and not the arrest of Bishop Trelawny, was the real occasion of the well-known chorus. The united and independent action of Cornwall on the side of the King during the great Rebellion was another instance of nationalism. The Cornish acknowledged Charles as their King and were not going to be dictated to by an English House of Commons, in spite of the fact that the boroughs of Cornwall returned a very disproportionate number of members to it. But for the treachery of a trusted agent—not a Cornishman—there would have been a Cornish national rising in 1715 in favour of him whom they almost unanimously held to be their rightful King, James III., and against the German Prince imposed on them by England. Whenever it may have been first consciously recognised, the separate national sentiment of Cornwall was very much helped in the days when ideas of nationality were in the balance by the existence of a separate and Celtic language, and down to the present day by the still existing, though much diminished, difference of jurisdictions. The title of " Prince of Wales," in every case separately conferred on the eldest son of the Sovereign, is only a titular honour. The hereditary office, as well as title, of " Duke of Cornwall," is even now very much more and, except for the Duchy of Lancaster, which is always merged in the Crown, is the only remaining example of a territorial as opposed to a merely titular Duchy. Its existence shows that it is not Cornishmen only who recognise the separate nationality of Cornwall. The Celtic language of Cornwall as a distinct spoken tongue has been disused for only about a century and a half. It would have been quite possible for the present writer to have met in his childhood with one who actually had heard it spoken, though as a matter of fact he never did. The nearest that he ever got to it was to meet more than fifty years ago with certain persons who had known isolated instances of people who could speak it. If the language may be said to be dead, the tradition of it, apart from books, is living, and its ghost still haunts its old dwelling in the forms of the vast majority of

Cornish place-names and an English dialect with many
Celtic words in it. There is no wish on anyone's part to
translate the Irish political expression "Sinn Fein" into
Cornish, to agitate for Home Rule for Cornwall, in any
way to disparage the neighbouring Kingdom of England or
to foment disloyalty to England's King or to the British
Empire. The whole history of Cornwall is against any
such ideas, and the Royal Letter in so many of our Cornish
churches is a testimony of Cornish loyalty, which has not
deteriorated since the day when the Cornish Host fought for
King Charles in 1643. Yet Cornwall is undoubtedly a
nation and though it no longer speaks a Celtic language, its
national consciousness and characteristics are still as Celtic
as those of the many Irishmen, Scottish Highlanders and
Manxmen who have no Gaelic, the many Welshmen who
speak only English, and the many Bretons whose only
language is French. If Celtic nationality is denied to
English-speaking Cornishmen, it must equally be denied to
those many members of the other Celtic nations who speak
no Celtic language—which is absurd When Cornishmen
cease to recognize the existence of their Celtic heritage then
only will their Cornish and therefore Celtic nationality
cease. It is for the Old Cornwall Societies to see to it that
such a calamity never happens. And the Cornish Gorsedd,
which is an outward and visible sign of the full recognition
by Wales of Cornwall as a sister Celtic nation, and is largely
a result of the work of the Old Cornwall Societies, will,
if rightly guided, go far towards ensuring that the Celtic
Cornish spirit will never die. The Ex-Archdruid Elfed (the
Rev. Howell Elvet Lewis) has recently said that the Welsh
Gorsedd has really become the medium between academic
scholarship and popular culture. It is for the Cornish
Gorsedd to take up the same ideal, and since "popular
culture" in Cornwall, as in Wales, is necessarily in a great
measure Celtic culture, to turn it into the right channel,
which is not pageantry and ritual only, but something much
more serious and beneficial.

GWAS MYHAL.

WHO ARE THE CELTS & WHAT HAS CORNWALL TO DO WITH THEM?

IN order to explain what is meant by Celts and Celtic nations it will be necessary to go back to very early history and to tell rather a long story, which begins before the Celts had any separate existence.

Very long ago there appeared in Europe a people speaking what, using a generally adopted name, we may call the primitive or original form of the Aryan or Indo-European languages. "Indogermanic," written all in one word, is also commonly used, but is an inadequate term. They were a race of high intelligence and of great fighting and adminstrative ability, and had somehow developed a language which had in it the germs of the highest cultivation. It is perhaps characteristic that the word *Aryan* is derived from the Sanskrit and old Persian *Arya*, noble, and was originally applied to the ruling races of India and Persia. Where they originated is uncertain, and there have been various theories, one of the latest of which puts their original habitat in the district between Bohemia and the Carpathians, and when they came to be differentiated from other peoples is also unknown, but the present idea seems to be that their existence first became known as early as about 3000 years before the Christian era. This, however, is very conjectural. They were not very civilised compared with the Mediterranean races, but they had, as time proved, the potentiality of the highest civilisation. Somewhere about 2000 B.C. the Aryan hive, wherever it may have been, began to send out swarms. Some went eastward to Persia and India, some westward and southward to the Mediterranean area and to central, western and northern Europe, and with their superior fighting and organising ability they overthrew ancient civilisations, like the Minoan in Crete, and subdued those peoples who were in a civilisation no better than their own.

They probably were not great in numbers in proportion to those whom they subdued, but they became a ruling class or military aristocracy, and were able, more or less, to impose their language on the original inhabitants. It is quite likely that the languages which grew out of the primitive Aryan after the dispersion were affected in their development by the various non-Aryan tongues which they displaced, and that the general population of each country was largely non-Aryan in blood, with a certain infusion or flavouring of Aryan, which perhaps leavened the whole community, and an upper or ruling caste of purer Aryan race. In India, owing to the very definite caste system, this may be more clearly distinguished than in Europe.

Though language in not an indication of race so much as of social contract, it is usual and convenient to classify the Indo-Europeans by the groups or classes into which the original Aryan language became divided. Each group has marked characteristics of its own, which are found in a greater or less degree in the later sub-divisions, but all the groups bear tokens of a common origin. There are roughly speaking seven main groups. 1.—The Indian, of which Sanskrit is the oldest extant form and possibly the nearest of any to the purely conjectural original Aryan. 2.—The Iranian, now chiefly represented by Persian. 3 — The Slavonic and Lithuanian, which now nearly form two groups. 4.—The Teutonic, to which the grammatical basis of English belongs, though there is a large admixture in its vocabulary from the next group. German, Dutch, Frisian and the Scandinavian languages are more purely Teutonic, with a minimum of foreign elements, and Gothic, now chiefly known through Ulfilas's fourth century translation of the Bible, is the earliest known form. 5.—The Italo-Greek, which early divided into two branches, of which Latin and its contemporary congeners and modern derivatives form one, and Greek the other. 6.—The Celtic, of which presently. There are so many common points of resemblance in Gaulish, the oldest known form of Celtic, to Latin and other Italic Aryan languages, that it has been suggested that they had a common ancestor in an off-shoot from the parent Aryan stock, which may be called the "Italo-Celtic." 7.—The Skipitar or Illyrian, a group consisting now of only one language, spoken in Albania and in a few Albanian colonies of refugee descent in Italy and Sicily. It is probable that Armenian may also be claimed as Aryan. The speakers of all these groups have assimilated Aryan ideas, whatever their actual proportion of Aryan blood may be,

It has been found convenient in recent times to
divide the population of Europe, nearer Asia and Africa,
quite irrespective of language and race, into
" Mediterranean," " Alpine " and " Nordic " man, and no
doubt when the Aryans came into the pictuie these three
divisions held good, as to some extent they still do.
Mediterranean man was then the most civilised.
Civilisation, as we understand it, begins on and about the
Mediterranean, and in the Egyptian, Minoan, and
Mesopotamian cultures it had attained to a very high pitch
before the Aryans came in and gave it something of a set-
back. The Aryans had, no doubt, high qualities of their
own. It may, for instance, be claimed for them that it was
they who invented the idea of a " gentleman," a type not
very noticeable in what we know of the older civilisations.
But they were certainly in a much less advanced stage
than " Mediterranean " man, only part of whose civilisation
had spread to them. " Alpine " man in his pre-Aryan stage
had some culture, probably of the Neolithic and Bronze Age
sort, and " Nordic " man, though he had progressed into
what has been called the " food-producing " stage from the
merely " food-gathering " state of the savage, and had
perhaps arrived at the use of metal, was in the least civilised
condition of the three. It was " Alpine " man, after his
contact and mixture with the invading Aryan, who
developed into the Celt. Aryan civilisation and language
were probably mixed with those of the original " Alpine "
man and the result was the Celts. We, of course, do not
know what were the proportions of the mixture or how long
it took to effect. Archæology has given us some ground on
which to reconstruct the pre-Aryan culture of " Alpine "
man, but of his language we know nothing, and what little
can be conjectured from possibly non-Aryan elements in the
Celtic languages is little better than pure guess-work.

The Greeks, who are not very early in mentioning them,
were inclined to lump together all peoples fairer-haired than
themselves, who lived north of the Alps, as "Keltoi" and they
probably never came much into contact with the still fairer-
haired " Nordic " man. When more exact details are
given by Greek or Roman writers and when we add to these
the measurements of skulls, we may gather that the Celts
were mostly round-headed, with broad faces, hazel or grey
eyes, light chestnut hair and broad shoulders and were
rather above the middle height, and when we get to a
period when they are mentioned in authentic history we find
them occupying a middle place, physically as well as

geographically, between the shorter, darker and sallower-complexioned "Mediterranean" men and the much taller, long - headed, long - faced, lighter - haired, blue - eyed "Nordic" type.

Archæology gives us data about the Celts perhaps in the Bronze Age and certainly in the Iron Age, but they are not found in the Neolithic or late Stone Stage. They sometimes, but not always, cremated their dead—a very general Aryan practice, found in places as far apart as the British Isles and India, and used by at any rate the upper or more purely Aryan classes of Rome—and they buried their ashes in isolated round barrows, or later in collective cemeteries. They were, at any rate in their later period, highly skilled in ornamental metal-work, and to them belong many of those beautiful bronze objects, often set with lumps of red coral or later with red enamel, and decorated with spiral devices, which have so frequently been found in the form of shields, horse-trappings, pins, brooches, bracelets and other things. There was developed in the " Late Celtic " period, as the Museums rightly describe it, a very beautiful and distinctively Celtic art, which later on, coming in contact with what is usually called Byzantine, but is really the art of the Roman Empire from the end of the 4th century onward, itself developed into the style which found its highest exemplifications in such wonderful illuminated manuscripts as the Book of Kells and the Lindisfarne Gospels,—the latter Anglo-Saxon under Celtic influence,—and is wide-spread in the many varieties of interlaced ornament known as " Celtic twist," examples of which are not uncommon on Cornish crosses. They appear from historical evidence to have been fine fighting men and good horsemen, brave and warlike,—perhaps rather too quick-tempered and quarrelsome, — the remains of their fortresses show that they had a more than rudimentary knowledge of military engineeering, and we find that they were great talkers and orators, with a high appreciation of poetry. Of their religion archæology tells us nothing—one would not expect it—but when Roman writers begin to talk about them, they, at any rate in Gaul and Britain, seem to mix up two different elements in it, the usual Aryan polytheism, with a number of gods whom, after their usual practice, which probably had a good deal more of truth in it than they knew, the Romans identified as their own gods under other names, and that mysterious and rather esoteric thing, Druidism, of which, considering how much has been written about it, we know very little. It would seem possible that Druidism was in its origin a pre-Aryan religion with a good deal of magic and perhaps some rudimentary philosophy in it, which the pre-Aryan but Aryanised " Alpine " men retained and many of the purer Aryans adopted in addition to their own polytheism, and modified considerably. There was no exclusiveness about Pagan religions. They were very " undenominational," and there was no reason why the same man shonld not belong to and practice two or more different cults. Whether, as polytheists or Druids, the Celts made use of the perhaps Neolithic or, as some think, Bronze Age, stone circles, cromlechs and menhirion for religious purposes, we have no means of knowing.

Authentic history of the Celts does not begin until about the fifth century before Christ, but before that there is archæological and philological evidence that their sphere of influence extended from what is now Austria, if not farther east, to Ireland. It has been held that the Bronze Age people, who used the leaf-shaped swords, invaded Britain probably in the ninth century B.C., but made no permanent settlement there, passed on to Ireland and were ancestors of the Goidelic or Gaelic-speaking Celts, but some hold that there was no such invasion and that the bronze weapons were peaceful importations. The great early Iron Age cemetery at Hallstatt in the Salzburg district of Austria, perhaps beginning a century later, is pro'ably Celtic, and the finds there are of such importance that the name has been applied to a particular stage of Iron Age culture, wherever found, just as " La l'ène," the name of another great Celtic cemetery, on the Lake of Neuchâtel in Switzerland, is used for the Late Iron Age of some three or four centuries later. Certain it is that at a very early date the Aryan peoples had made permanent settlements in what are now Austria, Tyrol, Switzerland, South Germany, France and Spain and had mingled with the pre-Aryan population so as to form that more or less homogeneous body which we call the Celts. This mingling was actually recognised in the name " Celtiberians " applied to the inhabitants of Spain, where perhaps the Iberians predominated, where the place-names which are not Roman or later are, with a few Celtic exceptions, mostly pre-Celtic, and a language which may possibly, but not certainly, represent the ancient Iberian still survives in the Basque provinces. There are many place-names in Austria, Switzerland, and South Germany and of course in France, which are of Celtic origin, not only of hills, rivers and other natural features, but even of towns. There cannot be said to have been a Celtic Kingdom or Empire over all these lands, for the Celts seem never to have been united under one head. There were probably many tribes, clans or kingdoms, and though they might occasionally combine against a common enemy, they could also quarrel a good deal among themselves. This want of unity has always been a source of weakness to the Celts. We may find on a small scale in the history of the Highland clans as late as the middle of the 18th century a state of things which probably prevailed over the vast extent of Celtic territory two and three thousand years before. The Celts first came into contact with Mediterranean civilisation east of Spain chiefly by plundering raids, and in only two cases, Cisalpine Gaul in North Italy and Galatia in Asia Minor, both in really historic times, did these develop into at all permanent settlements.

The earliest known writer to mention the Celts at all is Herodotus, who was born in B.C. 484, and he evidently knew very little about them. Speaking twice over (II. 33 and IV. 49) of the river Istros or Ister, now the Danube, he says that it rises in the country of the Celts, who live outside the Pillars of Hercules (now the Straits of Gibraltar), close by the Kynesii or Kynetes, whoever they may have been, and are the most western people of Europe. He is right about the source of the Danube, though he made a bad guess at where it was, for the Black Forest, where it actually rises, was certainly in Celtic territory when he wrote. The older Greek writers after Herodotus only knew the Celts or Gauls as occasional raiders from the North and say very little about them, and it is not till we come to late people, like Plutarch, Strabo, Diodorus Siculus, Ptolemy and others of the Roman Empire period, that we get much about them. The Romans, who came into more direct and frequent contact with them, have a good deal more to say. It would seem that their idea was that about the seventh century B.C. the Gauls began to concentrate in what is now France, which, with North Italy, acquired somewhat later, became their most important country. In 391 B.C. a large raiding party of the Senones, a Gaulish tribe, invaded Italy beyond the Apennines under one Brennus, burned Rome, and were eventually driven or bought off. More than a century later another host under another Brennus— perhaps the name is what in Welsh is *Brenhin*, king, or it may be the equivalent of *bran*, raven, a sort of " totem" name, or it may not—invaded Macedonia, penetrated into

Greece and sacked the temple of Delphi. They were driven off with great loss and some of those who got away settled in Thrace and Dacia, while others crossed over into Asia Minor and founded the state of Galatia, where as late as the second half of the fourth century of our era St Jerome claimed to have heard the Celtic language of the Gauls spoken. How Rome gradually absorbed the Celtic territories of Spain, Gaul, Rhætia, Vindelicia, Noricum, Pannonia, Galatia and Britain into its Empire, to their great and lasting good, belongs to general history. The Celts in all these countries, though, in Gaul especially, they gave a good deal of trouble, submitted eventually to Rome, and they must have been in a much more advanced stage of civilisation than appears superficially, and one not far removed from that of the Romans, if they could so readily assimilate Roman civilisation and adopt the Roman language, as they did. The great and wonderful fact of the Roman Empire, lasting effectively from the accession of Augustus to supreme power in B.C. 29 to at least the taking of Rome by the Goths in A.D. 410, draws a broad band across the page of the world's history. After it nothing was the same as it had been before it. During its period thos e in it who had been Celts became effectively Romans, and on the continent completely and in Britain, because the absorption had not been so complete, only partially, the Celtic languages died out in favour of Latin. It is not known when Gaulish finally ceased to be spoken. St. Jerome. who may or may not have known any of it, states that he had heard it in the neighbourhood of Trèves and notes its similarity to what he heard later in Galatia, but the Celtic tongues of Gaul, Spain, North Italy and what are now South Germany, Switzerland and Austria died out absolutely, leaving only place-names and a few inscriptions to show that they had ever existed and, except where German later took their place, gave way in favour of more or less corrupted Latin, which gradually differentiated itself into what we now call the Romance languages and those who spoke them ceased to be the "Celtic" and became the "Latin" races. There is hardly a trace of Celtic influence, except possibly in phonology, in any of the derivatives of Latin now spoken by those whose ancestors were Celts, and from the fall of the Empire onwards the name of "Celt" could only be applied to some of the inhabitants of the British Isles and to a British colony in North-Western France. The great Celtic territory, which stretched right across Europe, had shrunk to the "Celtic fringe."

Gaul and the Celtic territory in Switzerland, South
Germany and Austria had been subdued and the inhabitants
largely Romanised under Julius Cæsar, Augustus and
Tiberius, B.C. 58 to A.D. 37. Cisalpine or North Italian
Gaul had become a Roman pro.ince as early as B.C. 222 and
the Gaulish language soon died out there, though plenty of
Celtic place-names survive to this day. Galatia also was
annexed fairly early. The British Isles down to the time of
Claudius remained practically unaffected by Rome, for the
two invasions of Julius Cæsar in 55 and 54 before Christ
had pro.luced no effect of any .importance. At that time
these islands were, but for possible survivals of uncivilised
aborigines in forests and mountains, entirely. Celtic, but
were inhabited by two different sort of Celts. At some
unknown period, but probably very early, the original Celtic
language had divided itself into two very distinct branches,
which we now call " Goidelic " and "Brythonic," and this
division holds good to the present day. When the Celts had
separated from the hypothetical Italo-Celtic branch they
made in their language certain phonetic changes which
were not made by the Italic branch. One of the most
noticeable of these was the loss of an original Aryan initial
P. This was common to all the Celts, but is not found in
the other Aryan languages, though some, like the Teutonic,
aspirated P into F. Thus the Sanskrit *piti, pitri*, Greek
patẽr, Latin *pater*, German *Vater*, English *father*, became
in old Irish *atar*, modern Irish *athair*. The Latin *plenus*,
full, is represented by the Irish *lán*, Welsh *llawn*, Breton
leun, Cornish *len*. And there are so many cases of this that,
when one finds an Irish word beginning with P, one may be
almost always sure that it is a comparatively modern
borrowing from some other language. The most noticeable
difference between the Goidelic and Brythonic branches is
that Brythonic has regained an initial P, not indeed where
it occurred in the original Aryan, but as a substitute for the
Old Celtic initial sound QU, which Goidelic has retained as
C or K. This change is found otherwise than as an initial.
Thus, the well known Gaelic word *mac*, son, becomes *map*
in Welsh, Breton and Cornish. The old Irish were so
at'ached to an initial C instead of P that, when as
Christians they adopted certain words through Latin for
ecclesiastical terms, they made *Pascha*, Easter, into *Caisc*
and *Pentecoste* into *Cingcis*, and there are several more
instances of this change. Thus the Goidels have been
called "Q-Celts," and the Brythons "P-Celts," and the late Sir
John Rhys once made a rather ponderous Welsh joke, that in

order to distinguish between the two branches you must
"mind your Ps and Qs." Another change was between F
and GW. The original Celtic *windos*, white, became *fionn*
in Gaelic and *gwyn* in Welsh, and when St. Fingar and
St. Kieran came from Ireland to Cornwall, the Cornish made
their names into *Gwinear* and *Piran*. Another change was
that an old Celtic S was retained in Goidelic but often
changed into H in Brythonic. Thus, the river, which the
Romans made into *Sabrina* and we call *Severn*, is *Hafren*
in Welsh. There are other differences, which it is not worth
while to go into now, suffice it to say that Goidelic is
mostly a more archaic form of Celtic than Brythonic,
though it is easy to see that both come from a common
original. It is not a point on which there is any certainty,
but it seems probable that the Goidelic was the first wave
of Celtic invasion into these islands, and perhaps happened.
as has already been said, in about the ninth century before
Christ. There is nothing to show that they settled at all
permanently in South Britain, though if, as is not
improbable, the Picts were Goidels, they did settle in what
is now Scotland, and were there when the Romans came.
But most of them according to this theory passed on into
Ireland, perhaps attracted by the gold which was then found
there in some abundance, and as they could not get any
further, stayed there. All they seem to have done then in
what are now England, Wales and Cornwall was to leave a
good many of their leaf-shaped bronze swords and other
implements lying about for modern antiquaries to argue
about. It is, however, also possible that, as some think, they
came direct to Ireland, without crossing Britain, and that
the bronze implements got there as merchandise. They
probably called themselves by some name the nearest to
which we can get to is *Goidel*, and their language *Goidelic*.
Their descendants in Ireland, the Highlands of Scotland and
the Isle of Man still call themselves *Gaedheal* and their
language *Gaedhealg*, which we pronounced, more or less
correctly, *Gael* and *Gaelic*. The men of the Hallstatt
culture, who certainly came to Britain, were perhaps
Goidels, though they may have been Brythons, but it would
seem probable that the main body of Brythonic Celts, now
represented by the Welsh, Cornish and Bretons, came as a
later wave of conquest, probably not much before about 400
B.C., and were in the "La Tène" stage of culture. The
Gauls, as the scanty remains of their language show, were
probably of the Brythonic or "P" branch, though there
may have been some survivals of Goidelic Celts in the

middle one of Cæsar's three div'sions of Gaul, the country which Pliny calls "Celtica," between the Seine and the Garonne. The Belgæ, who lived between the Scheldt and the Seine were certainly "P-Celts." But all the prehistory of Celtic Britain and Gaul is very uncertain, and our ideas are in the melting-pot, which is appropriate, seeing that the best judges take pottery to be the surest guide to the movements of peoples.

When in A.D. 43 the Romans began and very soon completed the conquest of South Britain, the country was in the possession of many British tribes ruled by their own kings. Some of these, such as the Belgæ, in what are now Hampshire, Wiltshire and Somersetshire, the Atrebates, a Belgic tribe, in Berkshire and part of Hampshire and the Parisii in the East Riding of Yorkshire, bore names similar to those of Gaulish tribes and there is very little doubt that they were colonies of those. The Belgæ were certainly civilised, and so no doubt were the tribes of all the district from Kent to the Severn westward and to the Wash northward, the Trinobantes, Iceni, Atrebates and the rest. They had sett'ed governments, their own gold and silver coinage, and a fair amount of commerce and agriculture. The old idea of the his'ory-books, that the Britons habitually went about in the rather inadequate attire of a suit of blue paint and were nothing but savages, has long ago been exploded. Nothing except place-names and personal names remains of their language as it was when the Romans came, but these show that it was almost, if not absolutely, identical with Gaulish, of which we know enough to show that it was a fairly civilised language with a well organised grammar. Possibly there were more barbarous tribes in the hill-countries of Wales and in the North, but we have very little positive evidence of that. The Romans, with some initial difficulty, for the Britons put up quite a good fight, conquered the country and proceeded according to their wise custom to re-organise it as much as possible on native lines. The territories of the tribes became something like we now call "counties" or "shires" with their old capitals as county towns, Isca Dumnoniorum (now Exeter) for the Dumnonii, Isca Silurum (now Carleon-on-Usk) for the Silures, Venta Belgarum (Winchester) for the Belgæ, Calleva Atrebatum (Silchester) for the Atrebates and the rest, and there is good reason to conjecture that the heads of the old royal houses, when they became Romanised, may have developed into something between Lords Lieutenant and chairmen of county councils. But after nearly four centuries of what is commonly called " Roman occupation "—an incorrect expression, implying as it does subjugation to a foreign power, whereas a Briton of, say A.D. 250, would have rightly claimed to be as good as Roman as any Italian—the old tribal tradition had disappeared, all educated people and probably most others talked Latin and all national consciousness was Roman. The Celts of Roman Britain, like those of Gaul had ceased to be Celts and had become Romans. The Gauls never revived their Celticism—their Romanisaticn had gcne too far— but even there some memory of it must have survived, for as late as the end of the 4th century we find the poet Auscnius ((n ɼ lin entiɼ g a friend on being of the race of the Druids. In Britain the Romanisation was less complete. Parts of Wales and possibly Cornwall were never effectively occupied, the lower classes in some rural districts probably still spoke British, and the gentlemen, whether of British descent or not, had to know something of it. There was enough of a nucleus of Celticism left even in the Romanised part of Britain to revive, and the peoples of the whole of Ireland and a great part of Scotland were never touched by Rome, until Christianity in its Latin form came to them in the 5th and 6th centuries, but remained Goidelic Celts.

Until A.D. 410 Britain remained an integral part of the Roman Empire. It has usually been said that about that time the Romans left Britain. This is not historically correct. For some time troops had been frequently withdrawn to the continent, where they were wanted for various purposes. Magnus Clemens Maximus, the Roman Emperor who had jurisdiction over Gaul, Britain and Spain from 383 to 388, himself according to Gildas a Briton, though he was probably actually born in Spain, took over a large army to Gaul and it never came back. Constantine, the usurping Emperor elected in Britain in 407, who for a time made himself master also of Gaul and Spain, took over many more, and Britain was largely denuded of its fighting men. But the bulk of those who were left were Romans also in civilisation and language. Then came upon them more raids of Picts and Scots from west and north and of Saxon pirates from the east, and when they claimed their right to assistance from the central government, they were told to fend for themselves, for the central government had enough to do to protect Rome. Thus the Roman province of Britain was left derelict. For a time the Romano-Britons did defend themselves bravely. The old districts or counties seem to have become kingdoms again, though there is no evidence that the new kings and princes of Damnonia, Gloucester, Venedotia, Demetia, Powys and the rest were representatives of the pre-Roman royal houses. Sometimes an Emperor or War-lord was chosen over all the kings. Such evidently were Ambrosius and Arthur and several more, and for quite a long time Britain preserved its Roman character, though no imperial legate was sent to govern it or legions to help it.

The Saxons, who had hitherto only made plundering raids, began to come as conquering settlers about the middle of the 5th century. Unlike the Goths, Franks and others who invaded the continental part of the Empire, they had no great respect for Roman civilisation, and not being town-dwellers they had no use for the fine Roman cities, which with few exceptions they destroyed and left waste. The Romanised Britons put up as good a fight against them as their ancestors had made against the Romans, and the Saxons had by no means a " walk over." The story of Arthur, himse f quite as much a Roman as a Briton, though largely mixed with legend, shows plainly that after the great battle of Mons Badonis or Badon Mount the check to the Saxons was very complete, and it was nearly fifty years before they gave much more trouble to the Romano-Britons. But though the Roman character was preserved for some time, and a knowledge of Latin, as is shown by inscriptions and by the very Roman colouring of the Latin works of the 6th century Gildas, survived, there soon came a reversion to Celticism, which no doubt began in Wales and Cornwall and in the North, where the Romanisation had been less complete and the British language had survived in the mouths of at any rate the lower classes. What became of the Romano-Britons of south-east Britain who were not wiped out by the Saxons we do not know. Some no doubt fled westward and in some cases became the leaders of the Britons who were still holding out. This may be inferred from the remarkable prevalence of Latin names among the leaders down to quite a late period. But it is clear that there were not enough left of the thoroughly Romanised classes to rebuild a Roman civilisation, which, as in Gaul, should absorb the Teutonic conquerors, and so no Romance language has grown out of the Latin once spoken in Britain, as French grew out of the Latin of Gaul, and what was left of it was absorbed by the revived Celtic or replaced by Saxon. The Neo-British, which uplifted itself in the sixth century, was not quite the same thing as the pre-Roman British. The latter was a highly inflected and perhaps even a cultivated language. The new form had deteriorated in the mouths of the uneducated and had lost much of its elaborate inflexions, besides receiving a large infusion of Latin into its vocabulary,—there is a great deal of transmogrified Latin, not always easy to recognise, in Welsh, but the basis was Celtic, and so was what was left of the grammar, though if Caractacus or Cymbeline had been resuscitated in the sixth century and introduced to Taliessin or Llywarch Hen, they would prob ibly have had to fall back upon Latin if they had wanted to talk to each other. The language that arose became a very fine one and there have come down to us Welsh poems said to be of the sixth century, some possibly genuine, though we have them as somewhat modernised in the 12th century—those of Taliesin, for instance—which are really of great merit, and it is curious that their metres are largely founded on Latin metres imperfectly understood, and these metres have been used continuously for Welsh poetry ever since, though not for Cornish and Breton. The late Sir John Rhys, Professor of Celtic at Oxford, has shown rather convincingly that the very ancient and for epigrams still very popular Welsh metrical form known as the " Englyn Unodl Union " or one-rhymed stanza, is a distinct reminiscence of the Latin elegiac couplet of hexameter and pentameter.

In the middle of the sixth century the territory in the hands of the Britons, Romanised or otherwise, continued without a break, except of course the Channel, from the Clyde to the Loire. The kingdom of the North, later to be much diminished and called Strathclyde, extended into Cumberland, Westmoreland and Lancashire, and at the boundary of the last joined that of Powys, which included parts of North Wales, Cheshire and Shropshire. Westward of Powys was Gwynedd or Venedotia, the rest of North Wales, and southward were Dyfed or Demetia the western part of South Wales, and Morganwg or Gwent, composed of Glamorganshire and part of Monmouthshire. There were also the small principalities of Erging and Ewyas (in Herefordshire and Monmouthshire), Brecon, and Gloucester, as well as the little outlying kingdoms of Elmet and Leodis, from the latter of which comes the name of Leeds, in what is now the West Riding of Yorkshire. South of all these and extending to the Channel was the great kingdom of Damnonia, which included Cornwall, Devon, most if not all of Somerset and perhaps some of Dorset and Wiltshire. Beyond the sea was Armorica or Letavia, soon to be called Britannia Minor, or Brittany, which had at some period in the fifth century - the exact date is unknown—been colonised by Celtic speaking Britons, refugees from insular Britain. Of these Damnonia was certainly the most important, and kings or members of the royal house of Damnonia, Ambrosius, Uthyr, Arthur, and Constantine were the leaders of all the Britons for a period of nearly a hundred years. The probability is that those of the part of that kingdom eastward of Exeter had been more thoroughly Romanised than the people of Wales and the North and that its kings came of a family that had been great even before the connection with Rome was severed. Intercourse between all these kingdoms was complete. Though each was under its own king and those kings sometimes quarrelled and fought, they were all Britons together, and probably all called themselves so, though none except those beyond the Channel have retained the name— the modern use of it is another story. Even Asser, as late as the time of Alfred the Great, speaks of " Britannia," meaning Wales, and " Saxonia," though he also contrasts " Cornubia et Saxonia." Perhaps some old-fashioned people, like Gildas, still called themselves " Romans " and preferred to talk Latin, but Celtic in its Neo-British form had gained ground immensely and there was one British speech from the Clyde to the Loire, though even then there was a tendency to two dialects, the northern, now represented by Welsh, and the southern, which became Cornish and Breton. With the language came, no doubt, a revival of other Celtic characteristics, and what was later to develop into a national consciousness, which is so important a factor in determining what constitutes a nation, was rapidly ceasing to be Roman and becoming Celtic British again. Outside this undoubtedly British district and much further east there were some isolated Romano-British fortresses or communities which still held out, had probably not yet reverted to Celticism, and probably never had a chance of doing so. In 571, as we learn from the Anglo-Saxon Chronicle, Cutha or Cuthulf fought the Britons at Bedford and took Lygeanbirg, which is probably Leighton in Bedfordshire, Aylesbury in Buckinghamshire and Bensington and Ensham in Oxfordshire, so the Saxon occupation even of the East Midlands had not yet become very complete.

In 577 the Saxons became active again. Under Cutha and Ceawlin they fought a battle at Deorham (Dirham in Gloucestershire), and killed three British Kings, one of whom, called in the A.S. Chronicle "Condidan," whose name is possibly the Latin *Candidianus*, may perhaps be identified with Cynddylan ap Cyndrwyn, about the destruction of whose city—perhaps Uriconium in Shropshire —Llywarch Hen, the six century bard, composed one of the grandest of Welsh laments, and another, "Farinmeail," is probably the Fernmael of the Welsh genealogies. Then the Saxons took the fortified Roman cities of Gloucester, Cirencester and Bath, and having reached the Severn, divided the Britons of Damnonia from those of what we now call Wales. The Anglo-Saxon Chronicle, after its usual fashion, leaves it to be implied that the Wessex men did all this without any assistance. But Geoffrey of Monmouth tells another story, which he evidently did not invent, that Gormund, King of what he calls the "Africans", came over from Ireland with a large army to help the Saxons. Gormund is a Teutonic, not an Irish name, and Geoffrey's mention of "Africans" shows that he got his story from some original source in which Gormund's men were described as "Dubh-Ghall," black foreigners, the common Irish expression for Danes. The only black foreigners that Geoffrey had ever heard of were "niggers."* Very soon after the battle of Dirham the Saxons pushed the Welsh frontier back along its whole length to where it is at present and probably soon obtained possession of all the kingdom of the North as far as what is now Cumberland. The rest of that kingdom, which included Cumberland and Strathclyde, the western part of the country from the English border to the Clyde, remained as an independent Celtic state until in 945 it was conquered by the English King Edmund, who handed it over to Malcolm I., King of Scots.

Thus by the early seventh century there came to be three separate Brythonic Celtic countries in Britain and one across the Channel, and three of them are Celtic to this day. They were, beginning at the north :—

1. Strathclyde and Cumbria, which lost its independence in 945, but retained its British language to some extent down to the thirteenth century. The Strathclyde Britons, like the Welsh, called themselves, *Cymry*, or *Cumbry*, which is probably what in Gaulish

---

*This was first pointed out by the late Mr. Albany Major in his "Early wars of Wessex."

would be *Combroges*, compatriots, *com* having the same force as in Latin and *broges* being an inflected plural form from *broga*, Welsh, Cornish and Breton *bro*, country. The name still remains in that of *Cumberland*. It was nothing to do with *Cimmerians*, as has often been alleged. Apparently they soon lost all individuality after their annexation to Scotland, and those south of the Border, in Cumberland, seem to have been eventually largely exterminated and their places taken by Danes and Norsemen, to which type rather than to the Celtic the present inhabitants for the most part belong. There are still plenty of Cymric place-names in both Strathclyde and Cumberland and a good many in Westmorland and Lancashire, and those that have been superimposed are more Scandinavian than Saxon. Cumberland, except for a short interval in the reign of William the Conqueror, remained nominally part of the Scottish Kingdom until 1237. The Celticism of Strathclyde and Cumberland is absolutely dead and the inhabitants of this ancient division have long ceased to be Celts or to count themselves as anything but Englishmen and Scotsmen.

2. Wales or Cymru. This country was divided into several more or less independent kingdoms, Gwynedd, in North Wales, the very much reduced Powys, also in North Wales, Demetia or Dyfed in western South Wales, Morganwg or Gwent in Glamorgan and Monmouthshire, Brecon and some others. Eventually these settled down into the kingdoms or principalities of North Wales or Gwynedd and South Wales or Deheubarth (literally, "south-part"). After the Conquest of 1066 the Normans took possession of Deheubarth and their castles are all over the place there, but the people, except for the English and Flemish colonies in Pembrokeshire, Gower, etc. remained Celtic in speech and character. The languages and literatures of Wales and of Strathclyde and Cumbria were in common in the early period and it is not always easy to tell to which of these two countries certain of the possibly genuine early poems belong. There was also a good deal of migration to and from the two. The story of Cunedda, who came from the North— according to the current legend before or about the time of the final separation of Britain from the Empire— and drove out the Irish and Pictish invaders from North Wales, tells of one of these migrations, and the Life of St. Kentigern or Mungo, who went from Strathclyde to St. Asaph and then back again to Glasgow, shows how close a connection there was between North

Wales and Strathclyde in the sixth century. The Britons
of Wales adopted the same national name, *Cymry*, as those
of the northern Kingdom. Until the time of Edward I.
North Wales under its own Princes remained nominally
independent, but in 1283, after a brave resistance, it was
finally subdued as regards government. Though the King
of England became also King of Wales and created his
eldest son Prince of Wales, neither he nor any of his
successors succeeded in getting rid of the Celtic character
or language of the Cymry, and Celtic they have remained,
through periods of great discouragement, to this day, and
have gone on developing a culture of their own, especially
as regards their really fine and highly cultivated language
and literature, quite independent of and hardly at all
influenced by anything English, and for centuries practically unknown to Englishmen. There have been ups and
downs in this culture. The great " Celtic revival " of the
twelfth century, which from Cornwall, Brittany and Wales
influenced the literature of England, France and Germany
so much, was followed by a period of depression. Yet in
the 14th century Dafydd ap Gwilym, an exact contemporary
of Geoffrey Chaucer, was perhaps as fine a poet as any in
Christendom, except his other contemporary, Petrarch.
Since his time, though Wales has produced no really first-
class poet, it has, by means of the Eisteddfodau and
Gorseddau and the competition and interest evoked by
them, produced a remarkably high average of literary
excellence, purely Celtic and hardly influenced at all by the
outside world. The frontier of Welsh and English has
altered singularly little since the seventh century. In
Radnorshire Welsh has died out, and in the south-eastern
part of Glamorgan it is certainly much less generally spoken
than it was fifty or sixty years ago,* but everywhere else,
except in the isolated English colonies in South Wales, it is
still going strong. A noticeable tendency to bilingualism,
especially among children, will have its effect and the more
generally useful language will no doubt eventually prevail,
but the Celtic spirit and national consciousness will be
immortal and the Cymry will not become Englishmen, even
when they speak English. The use of the convenient names
Welsh and *Wales* requires explanation. The Teutonic
tribes, whether Goths, Franks, Saxons or Germans, used the

*In the parish of Wenvoe (about six miles south-west of Cardiff)
which for more than 150 years has belonged to the family of
the present writer, a good deal of Welsh was spoken when he
stayed there in 1867. There is now none.

word *Welsh* in some form or other in the sense of *foreigners*, but chiefly to denote people of the Roman Empire. To this day in German one of the names for Italy is *Wälschland*, especially in the dialects of the German-speaking people on both sides of the North Italian frontier. The canton of *Wallis* or *Valais* is probably a Swiss Wales, though now the west part of it is French and the rest German. *Wallachian* or *Vlach* is an alternative name for *Roumanian*. *Walnut* is the " foreign " nut. The Saxons when they came here called the Britons *Wealas* and their language, whether Latin or British, *Waelisc*, as a matter of course, and the name stuck. Whether it is connected with *Galli*, Gauls, the nearest foreigners to the Teutons, is not certain, but it is possible.

3. Damnonia, with its capital at the Roman city of Isca Dumnoniorum, which we call Exeter (i.e. Isca-Chester) and the Britons fairly soon called *Carwysc*, was really the largest of the seventh century kingdoms and had been the most important. It took its name from the pre-Roman tribe of the Dumnonii or Damnonii, whose territory extended from the Land's End to a line drawn due south from about Bridgwater to the sea—in fact, nearly along longitude 3° east of Greenwich. What connection more than name and site there was between that kingdom and its ruling house and the tribe and its old chiefs there is no means of knowing, but probably there was none. The part of it east of the Tamar had been a good deal Romanised, though Cornwall had not, and the new kingdom under rulers with Latin names, perhaps descendants of families which had been great under the Empire, was probably the most civilised of the British kingdoms. There is little difficulty in believing that the inhabitants were largely reinforced by Romano-British refugees from south and south-east Britain. At its greatest extent, nearly to the end of the seventh century, Damnonia reached to the Mendips, if no farther, for Glastonbury was certainly in it. Cystennyn Gorneu (Constantine of Cornwall), Erbyn (Urbanus), Geraint (Gerontius) Salamon or Selyf, Cador, Constantine II., Geraint II., Blederic and Geraint III., were kings from about 450 to 710, though there is a gap between the last two which is not accounted for. Of the nine only two have Celtic names. The two Constantines were also leaders of all the Britons, as were Uthyr and Ambrosius, sons of Constantine I., and Artorius, whom we call Arthur, the son of Uthyr. After the battle of Dirham in 577 the general over-lordship of the Britons passed to the royal family of Gwynedd, and

Damnonia ceased to lead. In the time of Ina, King of Wessex, the Saxons began to encroach on Damnonia. St. Aldhelm, Bishop of Sherborne, who was a personal friend of Geraint III., King of Damnonia, to whom he wrote an interesting letter about the Easter controversy and the way that the Celtic clergy cut their hair—matters which perhaps we should not now think so very important—kept the peace between Wessex and Damnonia, but he died in 709 and in the following year Ina attacked Geraint and pushed his frontier back to Taunton. In 721 or 722 the Damnonians received help from Rodri Molwynog, King of Gwynedd, and the Saxons were defeated at "Heil" in Cornwall, in a battle of which characteristically the Anglo-Saxon Chronicle says nothing. In the reign of Cynewulf of Wessex (755 to 784) the Britons were pressed further and further back into Devonshire, but no details of battles are recorded. In 823 there was a battle between the Devon men, who by that time were evidently Saxons, and the Cornish at Gafulford, which is not, as has been supposed, Camelford, but Galford in Lew Trenchard, where at a forked road (*Gaflffordd*, in Welsh) the earthworks of the opposing armies may still be seen. (An original *Camelford* might possibly become *Gafulford*, but a reverse change is very improbable.) In 831 Egbert invaded Cornwall and in 835 a Danish fleet joined with the "West Welsh" in an attack on Wessex and Egbert defeated the two armies at Hingston Down, near Callington. Then we get no records until under 875 in the Welsh chronicles it is said that Durngarth, King of Cornwall, was drowned. He is perhaps the "Doniert" whose tombstone still exists in St. Cleer. During the reign of Alfred there was peace, and for some time before that the Saxons had had enough to do to hold their own against the Danes. There is a rather vague story that Athelstan, who became king in 925, subdued and annexed Cornwall. The A.S. Chronicle says nothing about it, but it speaks of his ruling over several kings, among whom was "Huwal West-Wala cining," who, I think, is more likely to be Hywel Dda, King of west South-Wales, than a King of Cornwall, as he has been assumed to be. Athelstan, however, is known to have turned the Britons out of Exeter, where no doubt they had inhabited the parishes still called after Celtic Saints, and to have set the Tamar for their boundary. The independence of Cornwall ended in the tenth century, but still the Tamar is the boundary of Cornwall and England. No distinctively Celtic Cornish literature exist, for the mediæval Cornish dramas and poem have nothing especially Celtic about them. They are only ordinary mediæval literature represented in a Celtic language. But it does not follow that there never was any. It is quite possible that the nucleus of the great Arthurian cycle of romances was Cornish, though from the eleventh century onward it had been worked over, first by Bretons, who were really descended from Cornish emigrants, and shared in the traditions of the mother-country, and later by the literary world outside of Celtia. Whether the story of Arthur was originally composed in early Cornish, or, like the chronicle attributed to the 8th century Nennius, in which the first known mention of him occurs, in Latin of sorts, there is no means of knowing. It is probable that the Damnonians kept up their Roman civilisation and to some extent even the use of Latin, apart from its ecclesiastical use, for a long time before both were superseded by the revived Celticism. About fifty names can be clearly made out on inscribed stones in Cornwall ranging in date from the fifth to the ninth century. Of these about 17 appear to be Latin names, and the inscriptions, except the Oghams at Lewannick, are all in Latin. In the manumissions of the 10th and 11th centuries in the Bodmin Gospels there are 14 names of Latin or Greco-Latin origin, besides 13 Biblical names, which probably came in with Christianity during the Roman period, but the great majority are either Celtic or Saxon. After the Conquest Cornwall, which was all that was left of British Damnonia, became an appanage of the English Crown, recognised always as a separate entity, and its Celtic language, with an infusion first of Latin and later of English and French vocabulary, which down to 1400 was probably spoken over the whole county, continued to be the language of a constantly diminishing number with a constantly receding linguistic frontier, down to the 18th century, and its Celtic character and the national consciousness which it acquired remain to this day.

4. Armovica, Letavia or, as it came to be called, Brittany, was colonised by Celtic-speaking Britons certainly as early as the 5th century, even if there is no truth in the story of the migration under Conan Meriadoc in about 384. In 460 a fleet of 12,000 Britons under one Riothamir, their King, came up the Loire and attacked the Visigoths, and the accounts of this expedition by the contemporary Sidonius Apollinaris and Jornandes are the earliest existing mentions of Britons in those parts. This incident may have been the origin of the legend of Arthur's expedition to France. The fact that they called two provinces of their

new country "Cornubia" and "Domnonia," and the equally
noticeable fact that the Brythonic language which they took
with them was that of the Cornubia and Damnonia of
Britain show whence they came. It is probable that for
some centuries Cornwall and Brittany had their language
and perhaps literature in common, and that there was
constant intercourse between the two countries. One finds
evidence of the latter in the Lives of the Cornish and Breton
Saints, and even down to the last days of spoken Cornish, a
Celtic-speaking Cornishman and a Breton-speaking Breton
could have conversed fairly easily, though neither of them
could have talked with a Welshman. In the course of
centuries the two languages drifted apart, but nothing like
so far apart as Welsh drifted from both, and just as there is
no doubt that American, the language of a very much larger
country, is nothing but a dialect of English, so it could
fairly be claimed that Breton is only a dialect of Cornish.
What language, if any, the Britons found in Armorica when
they went there we have no means of knowing. It may
have been Latin or it may have been a form of Gaulish,
which affected the British which they brought with them
and was one of the causes of that drifting apart from
Cornish. But there is reason to think that the Western part
of Roman Armorica was practically derelict, and that all
that they found there were perhaps some "fragments of
forgotten peoples," like those of Tennyson's "sunset land of
Lyonesse," more or less savage forest-dwellers. Descendants
of such possible pre-Breton, pre-Roman and even pre-Aryan
and pre-Iberian people still exist in Brittany in the
"Bigaudens" of southern Finistère. After many vicissitudes,
conquests by Franks and Norsemen and other troubles, and
periods of being divided into small principalities, Armorica
settled down into being, under its own line of Breton Dukes, an
independent Duchy, the western half of which was Breton-
speaking, and remains so to this day, while the eastern part,
which probably had a larger and Latin-speaking population
when the Britons came there, was French-speaking, though
Breton place-names are fairly numerous even there. This
independence was maintained until the marriage of Claude,
daughter of Duchess Anne of Brittany, to Francis I., King
of France, in 1532, so Brittany was the last independent
Celtic country, unless one counts Scotland as a whole as
Celtic. Properly it ought to have become independent
again on the accession of Henry IV. of France, who was not
descended from the Breton Ducal House, but it did not.
Not without a struggle the union was maintained. Curiously

enough the present senior representative of the ancient
Dukes of Brittany is the present (de jure) King of Bavaria,
who is also heir of line of the English and Scottish Royal
House of Stuart. More Breton is spoken than any other
Celtic language, its district, the departments of Finistère,
Côtes-du-Nord and Morbihan, is a large one, and there is
no doubt about the present Breton national consciousness,
even in the part where they do not now speak Breton, if any
but a conquering minority ever did. There is little or no
distinctively Celtic Breton early literature. The folk-songs,
poems and dramas that exist are all late, later even than
some of the Cornish literature, and in metre, style and
subject matter they are obvious imitations of French.
There are some vague traditions of Breton bards of early
date, but they are rather legendary and no authentic works
of theirs exist. Yet the folk-lore and some of the folk-
music are undoubtedly Celtic in type and the former is often
very like Cornish folk-lore. Making all due allowance for
the greater size of the country, the more primitive condition
of the people, the modern influence of France rather than of
England, the centuries-old difference of political jurisdiction
and the very marked difference in the religion of what is
now probably the most intensely Catholic district under the
French republic, Brittany is still the country which beyond
all others most resembles Cornwall in the characteristics
and mentality of its people, and the Breton language is the
nearest thing to Cornish that exists. To a Cornishman an
Englishman is a foreigner and so is a Frenchman to a
Breton, to whom, as many Cornish visitors, including the
present writer, have reason to know, a Cornishman is a
compatriot, and that, curiously enough, without prejudice
to the loyalty of each to his own political jurisdiction.

The Goidelic branch of the present Celtic nations differs
very much from the Brythonic in language and mentality.
Unlike the Brythons, the Goidels never " went to school
with Rome." The Roman Empire left the Goidelic Celts
almost entirely unaffected by its ideas of civilisation and
order, and it was not until in the early fifth century that
which had become the religion of the Empire came to them
that they were influenced by it perceptibly at all. With
Christianity came a certain knowledge of the Latin
language for liturgical and other religious purposes, but the
Goidels never took to speaking Latin, though until the
Reformation all of them used it for Church purposes, as a
large proportion of them use it still. Thus it is that the
three living Goidelic or Gaelic languages of Ireland,

Scotland and the Isle of Man have been very little affected by Latin, and having never, like the Brythonic Celtic, suffered a temporary eclipse and having never, like that, been relegated to the use of the uneducated only, while an educated upper class spoke Latin, Gaelic has retained far more of its Celtic characteristics, modern Gaelic has developed from Old Gaelic without an uncultured period, and the mentality of those who speak it is far less Roman than that of the Brythons. The Goidels owe nothing except their Christianity, and to some extent the art which came with it, to the Roman Empire, and their civilisation was developed independently of it. The victorious enemy of the Goidelic languages and mentality has not been Latin but modern English.

Again beginning at the north, the Goidelic Celtic nations are :—

1. The Highlanders of Scotland. In the earliest times of which we have any knowledge a great part of Scotland was inhabited by the people called Picts. It is not quite certain whether their language was Goidelic or Brythonic, for nothing remains of it except names of places and persons, and these are rather indeterminate. If there is, as is possible, a basis of historical truth in the vague legends of the "Ossianic" literature, common to Ireland and the West of Scotland, there were Gaelic-speakers in Scotland at a fairly early date, perhaps even before the Christian era. About the end of the fifth century we come to something more definite. At that time Loarn Mor and Fergus, sons of Erc, were leaders of a band of Scots from Dalriada (North Antrim) in Ulster, who settled in what became Argyll (*Eirthir-Ghaidhil*, the coast of the Gael) and established what was known as the kingdom of the Dalriada Scots. Eventually (in 844) Kenneth MacAlpin, King of the Scots, became also King of the Picts, and this united kingdom included most of what we now know as Scotland. In the year 900 four languages were spoken in Scotland, Gaelic chiefly in the north-west, Pictish in a good deal of the north-east and central part and in Galloway, British in what was left of the kingdom of Strathclyde, and English in part of the south-east. Probably the court language remained Gaelic until about the time of the Norman Conquest of England. Pictish died out or was probably absorbed by Gaelic, and the Cymric British of Strathclyde lingered on until perhaps the thirteenth century. But English gained ground very soon and by the 13th century became in its Scottish variety the language of the Lowlands, except in Galloway,

where Gaelic of a sort is said to have survived until the period of the Covenanter troubles in Charles II.'s time, and Ayrshire, where Robert Burns might have met with the last speakers of it, though we do not know that he ever did. In the Highlands Celticism in language, habits and mentality has survived until the present day. The linguistic frontier, except as regard Galloway and Ayrshire, has not really altered for four or five centuries at least, and though there is now only a small percentage which has no English, Gaelic is still the mother-tongue of the people of a great part of the country beyond the Highland Line, that is to say to the north and west of a nearly straight line drawn from near the head of the Firth of Clyde nearly to Ballater, and then west of a line not so straight to Nairn. This was, and in sentiment and consciousness still is, though all their legal jurisdictions were abolished after the rising of 1745, the country of the Highland clans, and it was that system which kept the Highlands so markedly Celtic for so long. Until about the end of the 17th century the literatures of Ireland and the Highlands were in common, and though the languages, practically the same, of both countries called themselves Gaelic, the Scottish form was commonly called by the Lowlanders "Irish" or "Erse." There were no doubt dialect differences in the spoken languages, but until the beginning of the 18th century there was little or no literary recognition of them, and those who wrote anything wrote in Irish and used the Irish letters.* Since then some amount of quite good literature of Scottish Gaelic, chiefly of poetry, has grown up, but the Highlander is and always has been a warrior rather than a literary man, and being essentially a gentleman he is more inclined to take his troubles fighting than to sit down and whine about them. "Old, unhappy, far-off things, and battles long ago" do come into what there is of his literature, but there is not very much of it. Yet it is probable that there are more well-educated or upper-class speakers of Scottish Gaelic than of any other Celtic language. Owing to the long survival of the clan system the Highland chiefs and lairds always lived among their people, spoke their language and took a part in their lives, and many of them do so to this day. Though it is probably not, as it was until the 18th century,

---

*The existing Scottish Gaelic translation of the Bible, made in the seventeenth century, is very Irish, and though it is well understood by Gaelic speaking Highlanders, it must seem to them even more archaic than the English Authorised Version seems to us.

the actual mother-tongue of many of the quite upper class, who go to English public schools and universities, there are plenty of them who can and do speak Gaelic.* It is noteworthy also that there is probably more Scottish Gaelic spoken in Canada than in Scotland.

2. The Isle of Man. This little almost autonomous country still has a Gaelic language. It is not known when it got there, but there were "Scoti" in "Mevania" as early as the 4th century Cosmography of Æthicus. It holds a middle place between Scottish and Irish Gaelic, nearer perhaps to the former. In 1875 the present writer made some enquiries about the state of the Manx language. At that time the population of the Island, exclusive of the town of Douglas, then, as now, a mere English sea-side watering-place, was 41,084. Of these, 12,340 spoke Manx habitually as their own language and 190 could speak no English. Children for the most part spoke English only. In one church, Kirk Arbory, there was a Manx service once a month. Now after more than half a century there are none who speak no English and few, if any, whose mother-tongue is Manx, though there are a good many who can speak it and it is being patriotically but artificially preserved. It is probably in the state that Cornish was in when Lhuyd came here in 1700. There is no literature of any importance, except one Ossianic poem preserved in a manuscript of 1789 and taken down from the recitation of an old woman at Kirk Michael. The rest consists of songs, hymns, carols, etc., of no literary value, and a fair number of translations from English, including the Bible, taken from the Authorised Version, the Prayer-book of the Church of England, part of Milton's "Paradise Lost," Bishop Wilson's sermons and some of his other works. Manx, as differentiated from Scottish and Irish Gaelic, does not seem to have been written down until Bishop John Phillips translated the Prayer-book in about 1628. The language is still used officially for translations of the laws of the Manx Parliament, and a service in Manx was held, with a sermon by the Archdeacon, during the Celtic Congress of 1921.

3. Ireland, the principal seat of the Goidels in the British Isles. Whence and when they came there is unknown, but it seems probable that they came from the part of Gaul called by Pliny "Celtica," that is to say between the Seine

and the Garonne, and that perhaps passing through Britain, perhaps not, some time about eight centuries before Christ, they went on to Ireland. They were, according to Mr. O. G. S. Crawford (Antiquaries' Journal, Jan. 1922), the people of the leaf-shaped bronze swords, but that has not been generally accepted. But we know next to nothing about those except from discoveries of weapons and other things attributed to that particular type of Bronze Age folk, and the first Goidels to come to Ireland may have been in an Iron Age state of culture. Probably they found pre-Aryan people in possession, subdued them and imposed their language upon them. The fact that the prevailing type in a great part of Ireland seems to be non-Aryan is probably due to the comparatively small number of the Aryan invaders, who remained for a time a ruling aristocracy, but were gradually absorbed by the lower aborigines, a process perhaps accelerated in quite historical times by the migration of so many of the aristocratic class to the western part of Scotland. The Romans made no attempt to annex Ireland, but it is not until about the time of the Roman annexation of Britain that we begin to get any definite information about the country, for the Irish traditions of the Fir-bolg, Tuatha De Danan, Milesians and the rest are not quite trustworthy history. Aristotle (c. 345 B.C.) and Polybius (c. 160 B.C.) knew "Ierne" by name as one of the "Bretanic" Isles, but they say nothing about the inhabitants. Strabo (c. 30 B.C.) describes them as savages and cannibals, with other unpleasing customs which we need not go into. Pomponius Mela (c. A.D. 45) speaks of them as uncivilised, ignorant of all virtues and quite devoid of religion. Solinus (c. A.D. 80) has a more interesting, though still unfavourable, account of them. In the Latin and Greek writers of the period of the Roman imperial power in Britain there is curiously little about Ireland, but what little there is seems to describe the "Scotti," as the inhabitants are called, as being in a low state of civilisation. This is perhaps an injustice. Judging from the genuine pre-Christian Irish literature, of which there is a good deal, though in a somewhat modernised form, they had developed a fairly high civilisation of their own, though it was different from that of Rome. When with the coming of Christianity the Irish came into real contact with Roman civilisation, they were by no means unprepared for it, and the conjunction of the two produced a very fine culture. St. Patrick came to the Irish in 437 or 438, bringing with him the Gaulish type of monastic Christianity which caught on at once, and before his death perhaps in

about 470, though some put it as late as 492,
the whole island had become Christian. There had been
a few Christians there before St. Patrick, but they had
produced very little effect. The Celtic literature, art and
learning which grew out of the combination of Roman
Christianity with pre-Christian Celticism was of a wonderful extent. There was a time, perhaps from the seventh to
the ninth century, when Irish culture seems to have been
the most advanced in Western Europe— which, however, is
but faint praise. But this is a subject far too large for the
present paper.* The invasions of the Danes in the ninth
and tenth centuries did much to destroy it, and though a
literary tradition went on, it never quite recovered. The
earliest documentary evidence for the Irish Gaelic language,
except for some very early Ogham inscriptions, is of about
A.D. 700. Until the partial conquest of Ireland by the
English, which began in 1169, it had been the language of
the whole country except for the Danish settlements of
Dublin, Waterford and elsewhere, which had come to an
end after the victory of Brian Boroimhe at Clontarf in 1014.
The English Pale, as it was called, parts of the counties of
Dublin, Louth, Meath, Kildare, Wicklow, Wexford. and
Waterford, soon became English, and down to the early
part of the nineteenth century a dialect of English of a very
archaic sort was spoken in some parts of it. Until the 19th
century Gaelic continued to be the recognised language of
all classes outside the English Pale. In 1801 four out of the
five millions of Irish spoke it. It had four dialects more or
less conterminous with the four province of Ulster,
Connacht, Munster and Leinster. Of these the Connacht
was held to be the best and the Leinster. which had come
more in contact with English, the worst. The Munster
dialect differs from the others in the position of the stress
accent, which, as in the Vannes dialect of Breton, is on the
last syllable, whereas in the others, as in Scottish and Manx
Gaelic, it is usually on the first. The decline and
discouragement of Gaelic really began after the Union of
the Irish Parliament with that of Great Britain in 1801 and
the introduction of English education, especially for the
Catholic clergy, and though down to that time a more or
less flourishing literature had been kept up, and it had even
been thought worth while to translate the Bible and the

---

*The best recent book on this subject is Professor Macalaister's
"Archæology of Ireland," though there are some points in it
on which the present writer presumes to differ.

English Prayer-book into it, the use of the language began to be discouraged by the Irish people themselves, and it tended to be confined to the lower classes, by a sort of linguistic snobbery. There has been in recent years with the modern Irish political aspirations an artificial revival of it and there are even attempts to introduce it and to have it taught in schools in districts where it has not been spoken for centuries. What the result of this patriotic attempt has been or will be it is not easy to say. Statements regarding its success appear to differ according to the political opinions of the narrator and one might like the movement better if it were less tainted with controversial politics. But Cornishmen though they may have no sympathy with the particular Irish political ideas and the hatred of England which are certainly among the feelings which have helped to bring about the revival of Gaelic, must sympatise with that revival in so far as it tends to preserve the Celtic character of Ireland, about whose present Celtic national consciousness there can be no doubt. The "Scots" or Goidels of Ireland, who, as Solinus tells us, crossed the Irish Channel in boats made of wicker (vimineis alveis) with a covering of ox-hide (tergorum bubulorum), made plundering raids and settlements on the opposite coast of Wales and probably in Cornwall also. Later, in the 5th and 6th centuries, as Christian missionaries, they made a different sort of raid, and came to Cornwall in large numbers under the leadership of St. Fingar (Gwinear), St. Kieran of Saighir (Piran) and others, bringing the enthusiastic monastic form of religion, which had been brought to them by St. Patrick, to wake up the slumbering and rather slack Romano-British Church, which they found in possession. They made religious settlements around the Hayle estuary, in Breage and Germoe, in Perran in the Sands and elsewhere, and, as they probably brought lay followers as well as clergy, the descendants of these settlers perhaps still go on. There are also some place-names in the Irish missionary sphere of influence in Cornwall which seem to be possibly Goidelic rather than Brythonic, but the Goidelic invasions of the fifth and sixth centuries produced no traceable effect on the Cornish language, which remained Brythonic to the end.

To sum up, it will be seen that there were four periods in the story of the Celts. 1.—The prehistorical or, as it has been called, the proto-historical period. Of this our knowledge is very conjectural, though quite reasonably so, and is founded almost entirely on archæological finds of implements of stone, bronze, iron, "cloam" and other materials, generally in connection with interments, but especially on the classification of pottery, which for the last few years has been held by the best judges to be, as yet, the one of the surest method of dating. Some light may also be obtained from a study of place-names. These are a clue to the distribution of the Celts. 2.—The first historical period, during which the Celts, though still independent, had come sufficiently into contact with the Greeks and Romans to be brought into their authentic history. The story of the end of this period shows the decadence of Celtic independence and the gradual absorption of the British and Continental Celts in the Roman Empire. 3.—The Imperial period, during which the Celticism of the Brythonic branch was in abeyance, but that of the Goidelic branch went on developing on its own lines. In this period Continental Celticism died out absolutely. What proved to be only the temporary Romanisation of one branch of the remaining Celts has never lost its effect on the language and mentality of the Brythons, and this has been largely the cause of certain marked differences between them and the Goidels, who were never Romanised. 4.—The period of a revival of Celticism, influenced by Romanisation, among the Brythons, after the connection with the Empire had ceased, and its continuance to this day, with the parallel continuance of a Goidelic Celticism, which having suffered no eclipse, has a far more continuous tradition. During this period what we now call the Six Celtic Nations developed, largely under the pressure of external enemies, and each acquired a differing national consciousness, aided beyond a doubt by the possession of a language of its own. Cut off from the general comity of European nations by languages which, however excellent in themselves, it was not worth the while of other people to learn, separated in everything except membership of one Church, the Celts of the Middle Ages kept themselves to themselves, influencing or being influenced by the general European culture very little, and so developed considerably on lines of their own, and this isolation behind that barrier of language continued long after the whole of Celtia had lost its independence. Now and then little bits of Celtic influence spread to other countries, as when St. Columban and other Irish monks came as missionaries to the Continent, waking up the somewhat somnolent Western Church in Christian Latin lands and introducing Christianity among hitherto Pagan Teutons, or again when with the curious

"Celtic Revival" of the twelfth century the literary "Matière de Bretagne," as the French poet. Jean Bodel, called it, the great cycle of Celtic romance with the Cornish Arthur as its centre, permeated all European imaginative literature for centuries. But for the most part the Celtic nations presented in a greater or less degree the very unusual phenomenon of isolated communities, sufficient unto themselves, and taking very little notice of the outside world. It is only fair to say that the outside world returned the compliment and took very little notice of the Celts, except when, as occasionally happened, their fighting men gave some trouble to those who had conquered them, but had not effectively subdued their spirit. The Bretons and the Cornish for various reasons, geographical, historical and political, and perhaps because the Romanisation of their South British ancestors had been more thorough, held themselves less aloof from the outside world than did the other Celts, and were never too unfriendly to their immediate neighbours, nor had they any grievances to allege against them. The circumstances of the two countries were very similar. In Cornwall Norman influence from 1066 onwards must have been very considerable, but the Normans there, with that singular adaptability which was one of their characteristics, soon became Cornishmen in sentiment, if not, perhaps, in language, and made common cause with their people whenever there was any common cause to make. A good deal of the same sort happened in Brittany with Norman, Angevin and other French influences. One must not say that Cornwall and Brittany were more cultured than Wales, but that they assimilated more of general European culture, and therefore were necessarily in some respects less exclusively Celtic. In spite of the fact that to this day there are more unilingual Celtic-speakers in Brittany than anywhere else, while in Cornwall there are none, the Celticism of the two nations, is very much the same, and their respective attitudes towards the outside world are very much alike. Wales, whose inhabitants descend from probably less effectively Romanised Britons, preserved its independence much longer than Cornwall, though nothing like so long as Brittany, but lost it by conquest, not, like Brittany, by peaceful and legitimate inheritance. It is therefore not wonderful that for a long time its attitude towards the foreigner was less friendly and it was much less influenced by non-Celtic culture, and the fine cultivation of its language and literature on native lines, unaffected by anything external except the Latin of the Roman Empire

period and to some extent by the Catholic religious ideas of
the Middle Ages and later by the Welsh Bible, has kept it
freer from external influence than Cornwall or Brittany to
this day. As for the Goidelic Celts they are to this day far
more purely Celtic in language—when they speak it, which
probably a great majority of them do not—and in mentality
than the Brythons of any sort. Historical events have
varied the respective attitudes of the Goidelic nations
towards the rest of the world, as represented by non-Celtic
Britain. The Manx are perhaps a negligible quantity in
that respect and with their complete " Home Rule " have
probably no attitude towards the outsider, except to welcome
him as a tourist. The Scottish Highlander has never been
conquered or annexed—on the contrary it was he who did
the annexing, for it is not a paradox but sober historical
fact, that the King of Great Britain reigns not only because
he can undoubtedly trace his descent back to Cerdic of
Wessex, Alfred of England or William of Normandy, but
also and principally by virtue of his descent from Fergus
son of Erc, who in the late fifth century first brought the
Scots from Erin to Argyll, whose descendant Kenneth son
of Alpin in 844 suceeded to the kingdom of the Picts and so
united Alba or Scotland under one king, and whose still later
descendant James VI of Scots succeeded in 1603 to the
Crown of England. The Monarchy of Great Britain is really
in its origin a Goidelic, a Highland Scottish Monarchy, and
the Highlander is perfectly well aware of that and so he has
no grievance, real or imaginary, and his attitude to the non-
Celtic British outsider is a perfectly friendly one, of which
the worst that one can say is that it is perhaps, quite rightly
in the circumstances, a little *de haut en bas*. Ireland was,
no doubt, once a conquered country, but of Ireland and its
attitude it is better to say nothing here, one way or the other,
for in that direction politics lie.